JESSICA HAGY

How to Be INTERESTING

(In 10 Simple Steps)

WORKMAN PUBLISHING · NEW YORK

Library of Congress Cataloging-in-Publication Data is available.

ISBN 978-0-7611-7470-7

Design by Lisa Hollander

Workman books are available at special discounts when purchased in bulk
for premiums and sales promotions as well as for fund-raising or educational use.
Special editions or book excerpts also can be created to specification.
For details, contact the Special Sales Director at the address below,
or send an email to specialmarkets@workman.com.

Workman Publishing Company, Inc.
225 Varick Street
New York, NY 10014-4381
workman.com

Printed in the United States of America
First printing February 2013

10 9 8 7 6 5 4 3 2

for Tyrel

(the most interesting person I know)

TABLE of Contents

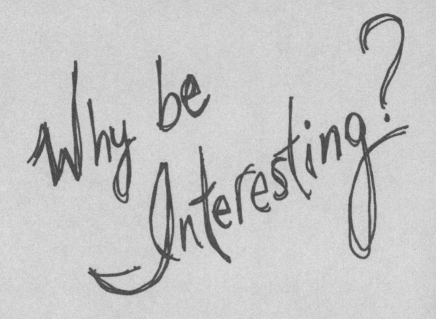

Why be Interesting?

★ To limit your regrets.

★ So you can respect yourself.

✯ In order to banish boredom.

✯ So that you can leave a mark, not a blemish.

✯ And most of all, because you can.

So Let's begin

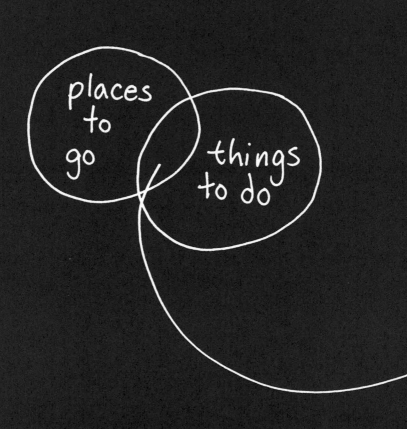

Go Exploring.

Explore ideas, places, and opinions. The inside of the echo chamber is where all the boring people hang out.

You

Them

TALK to

Humanity →

STRANGERS.

No one has seen exactly what you have.
No one has been to all the places you've
visited. No one feels just as you do.

Find out why.

ROLL
the
Dice.

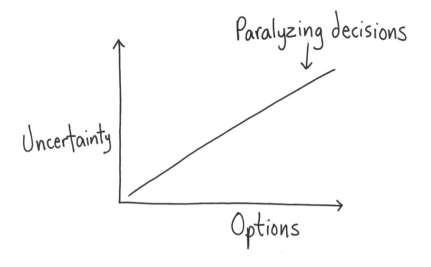

How far to go? Roll the dice. Seven blocks it is.
Take the train? Roll evens and buy the ticket.
Two dice can take you practically anywhere and
save you lots of time on unimportant decisions.
Keep them in your pocket. They'll help keep things
interesting.

UNPLUG.

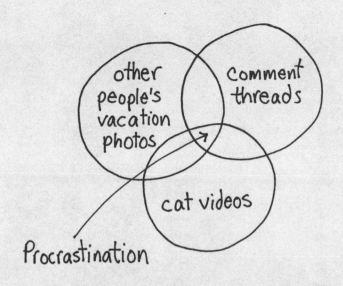

Without a map, you can find uncharted places. Be unreachable; you can talk to people on your journey. Miss a few updates from others, and discover yourself instead. Your gadgets are tethering you to a world you know very well.

Turn them off to explore new places.

Your comfort zone

Expose

Where the magic happens

Yourself.

To embarrassment.
To ridicule. To risk.
To strange events & conditions.
To WILD IDEAS.
To things that make you cringe.
To strange vistas & new sounds.
Trust me.
It'll be fun.

PLAY Devil's

How true
it is

Do the opposite of expected. Defend the
guilty. Question the pure. See which facts
are opinions and which opinions are facts.
There are many sides to every story, and
they all need to be told.

ADVOCATE.

People who believe it

* Myths, Advertisements, Political Promises
& Urban Legends

TAKE daily VACATIONS.

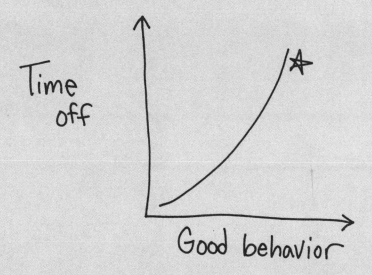

Time off (vertical axis)

Good behavior (horizontal axis)

✱ Parole & Vacations

If only for a few minutes. Stroll around
in the early hours, when the sunlight is a sliver.
Walk to a different mailbox. Read magazines
in a Laundromat. Shower in the dark.
Sip hot chocolate in an alley.
Reclaim your spare moments.

Anthropology

Become a

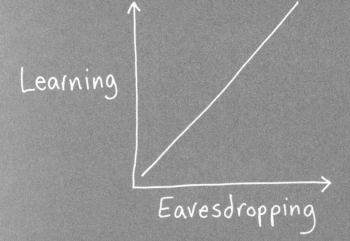

Learning

Eavesdropping

party
crashing

people
watching

SPY.

People watch. Eavesdrop.
Lurk. Loiter. Listen.
And you will learn the
secret codes of others.
Every day can be
an INTERESTING
recon mission.

SAMPLE flavors.

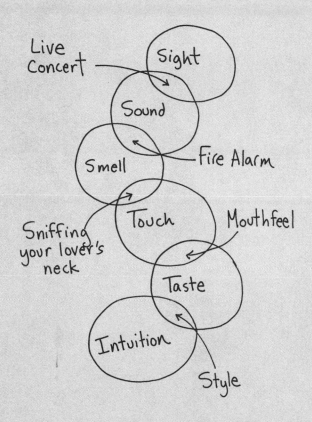

Live Concert → Sight
Sound
Smell ← Fire Alarm
Touch — Mouthfeel
Sniffing your lover's neck
Taste
Intuition ← Style

Open your mouth and say nothing, just observe.
How does the early morning dew taste?
What is the flavor profile of your commute?
Does someone else's detergent remind you of
childhood? Why do airports all smell the same?

Things
done

TWEAK the

Wake up before the alarm.
Steal moments between stoplights to
compose poems. Sneak off to a moonlit
spot when you'd otherwise be watching
something on a glowing screen.

• Satisfaction

• Regret

Time →

Schedule.

Work at night and play in the daytime.
Carve out hours for the dreams you've
been putting off.

There's always time to explore.
You get to decide when it is.

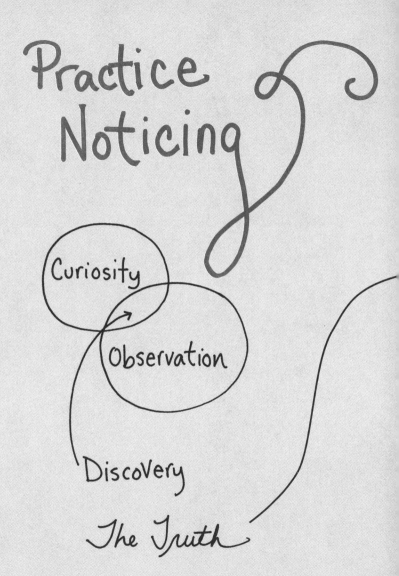

Practice Noticing

Curiosity

Observation

Discovery

The Truth

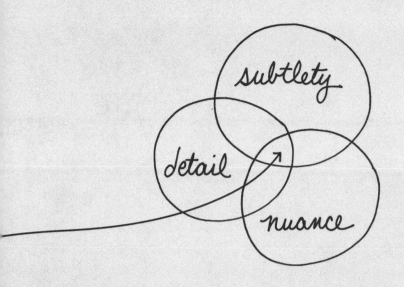

A faded sign. An eye patch. A broken lock. A photo
torn in half. A flat tire. A small scar. A spilled cup.
A pause when her lover's name is mentioned. Each
detail tells a story. And every room holds a thousand
details. Look for them.

Find the interesting stories.

Childlike
NOT
Childdish

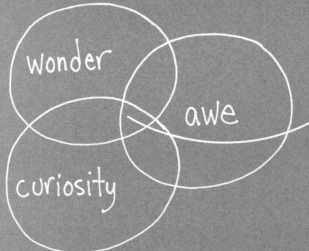

wonder

awe

curiosity

→ Eroded by
many classrooms,
cubicles & reality
TV shows

Look with open eyes.
   Remember how amazing the world was
      before you learned to be cynical.
See the neat things.
            The messy things.
      The funny things.
   Less CRANKINESS.
      More MARVELING.

Keep Asking Why.

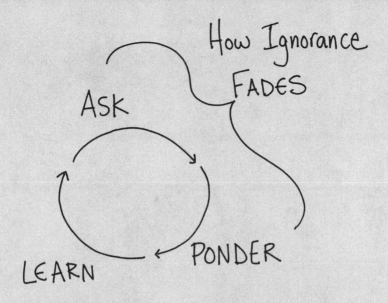

How Ignorance FADES

Ask

Ponder

Learn

Parents hate it when kids do it.

Why? Because.

Why? Because.

Why? Because.

And on and on. But try it. You'll be surprised at how quickly a simple *Why?* can turn into a fascinating *Because.*

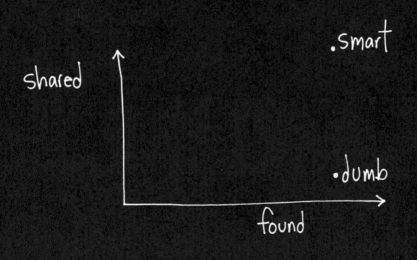

Step 2

Share what you Discover.

And be generous when you do. Not everybody went exploring with you.

Let them live vicariously through your adventures.

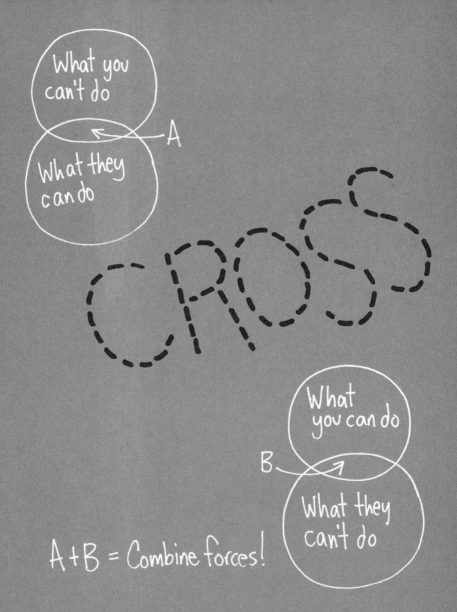

Pollinate.

You've got a thing, a
schtick, a specialty.
And so does everybody else.
Don't just associate
with folks who do what you do.
Seek out those with
different passions.
You'll be able to experience
exponentially more.

INSTIGATE.

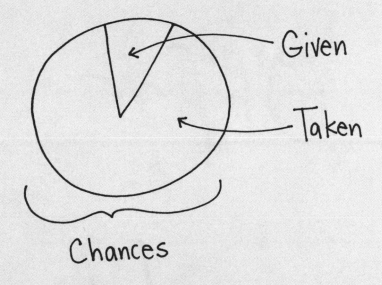

Given

Taken

Chances

Do not wait until tomorrow.

Say, do, or make it now. Go where you need to be.
Do not wait to be invited places. Host your own
parties. Do not sit by the phone. Pick it up. Spread
the word. Press the buttons. Buy the tickets and
enjoy the show.

Offer to Help.

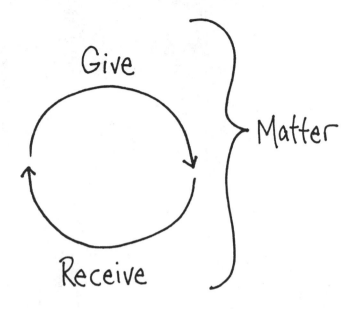

What you have is worth a lot. Seek out the people who need it. Know what you can do and tell people that you're willing to do it. They will treasure and remember you. Your time. Your talents. Your compliments. A seat at your table. A cup of sugar. A clean pair of socks.

The world needs whatever it is that you have.

what you
know

what other
people know

State   the

Less than you think

OBVIOUS.

What's known to you is often a mystery to others. Your old fact is someone else's new lesson. Your simple task is someone else's impossible chore. Your mind is full of treasures that no one else has seen. Pass them on. An idea shared is not diminished: It's multiplied.

don't

your
Voice

Wave hello instead of looking away.
Leave your perspectives in places where others
can find them. Put your work in the window,
not the basement.

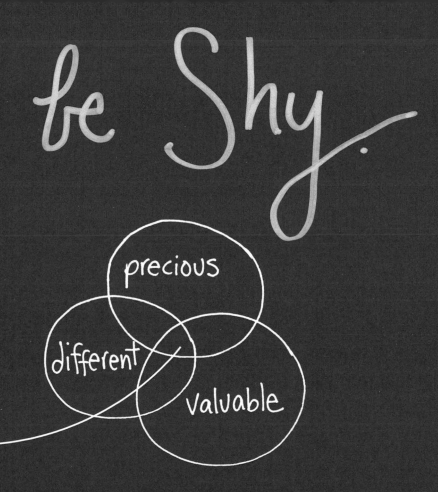

be Shy.

precious

different

valuable

Conversations begin with small steps toward
each other.

INVITE MORE THAN YOU R.S.V.P.

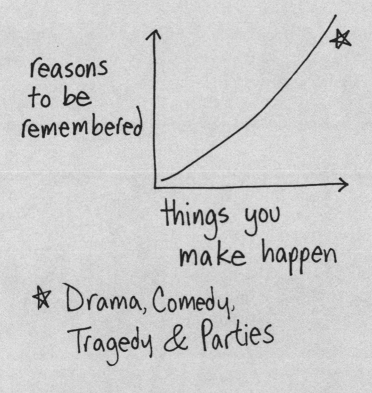

reasons
to be
remembered

things you
make happen

✻ Drama, Comedy,
   Tragedy & Parties

Bring others into your world. Let them play where
you hang out. Don't wait for invitations when you can
host. You can get something started as long as there
is at least one person you can invite.

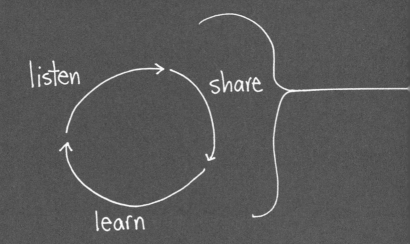

listen → share

learn

Be a link not

How
News
Gets
Made

an endpoint.

Don't just tell. Don't just listen.
Make introductions. Set up strangers.
Pass on what you know. This is how
ideas snowball into events. You can
be the fulcrum upon which an entire
community turns.

COMPLIMENT
Liberally.

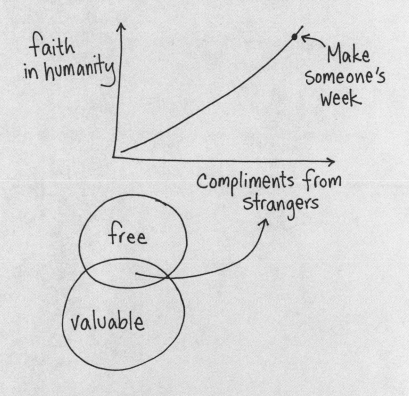

Kind words are quite precious and cost nothing;
it's surprising that they're so rare. Laud what you
enjoy. Praise the people who excel in novel ways.
Do it publicly and often.

Everyone needs more encouragement.

Good
Times

New People

•A

•B

Expand

A = The Group
B = The Morgue

the Group.

Never take in the welcome mat.
Keep the door open.
Make room for surprise
guests—you never know who
could show up.
They might be wonderful.
They might be
less than wonderful.
Hopefully, they'll be interesting.

Reach Out.

Introduce yourself

You are only one phone call, one letter, one text message, one email, one "hi there!" away from everyone. Yes, everyone.

The people you admire, who inspire and impress you, the people you love or would like to love—they are all so very reachable.

That's scary and comforting at the same time, isn't it?

CHAT.

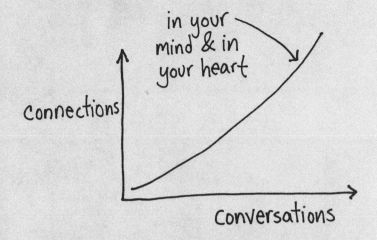

What are people talking about? Love? Loss? The weather? The magical? The mundane? What they have nicknamed their nether regions? The simple act of conversation can bring people together and expose you to interesting topics. So strike up conversations when you can.

Put your OWN

uniqueness of opinion

number of observations

Evidence of critical thinking

You see and you evaluate.

You read and you ponder.

This is human nature: We interpret

information as we absorb it.

SPIN
on it.

adventure

books

music

Fodder for diatribes

Well-constructed options add to
the original artifact.

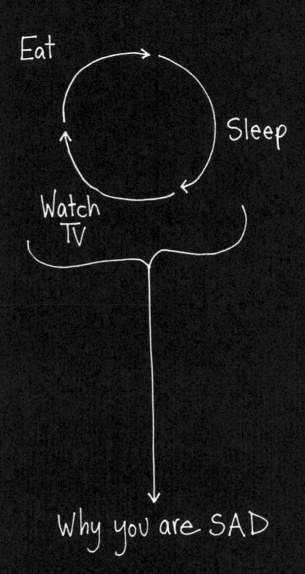

Do Something.
ANYTHING.

Dance. Talk. Build. Network. Play. Help. Create. It doesn't matter what you do, as long as you're doing it. Sitting around and complaining is not an acceptable form of "something," in case you were wondering.

Production Costs ↑ • Blockbuster

Real life is always in 3-D. It's always in high-definition. Outside is where the fascinating people and happenings are.

OUTSIDE.

.Skyline

.Sunset

$\longrightarrow$

Sense of Awe

It's where you'll find whatever it is
you're looking for.

Regret

Misery

. Being someone
other than
yourself

Do What

personal

political

economic

How you spend
your days

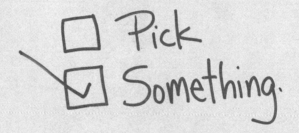

☐ Pick

☑ Something.

You Want.*

*yes, you

If it is unappetizing: Do not eat, date, or sign up for it. If the mere thought of it is depressing: Do not major in it, sit through it, or devote your life to it. If it is not important to you: Do not do it only because it is important to someone else.

You will thank yourself.

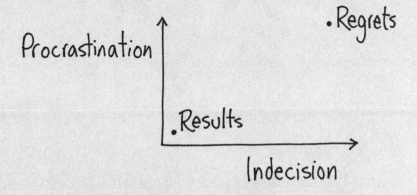

Not sure what to do with your day? Your life?
Your career? Frankly, it doesn't matter. Even the
most intricately organized plans can crumble.
And oscillating between options is a great way
to procrastinate your life away. Flip a coin. Spin a
bottle. Trust your gut. And off you go.

Involve

People
backing
you up

↑ •Prosperity

You'll need help. You'll need advice.
You'll need allies. So you have to tell
someone how you feel and what you're up to.
Let people in on what you're doing.

OtherS.

.Secrecy

→

Fear of failure

They will champion and support you more
than you ever imagined, and mock you less
than you fear.

SIGN UP.

Luck, Skill & Daddy's Money

Showing Up

Success

Join a club. Take a class. Volunteer.

Have a party. Take a meeting.

What we do shapes who we are.

Be someone who's been there, done that, and

wants to do new things tomorrow.

Earnestly ENJOY yourself.

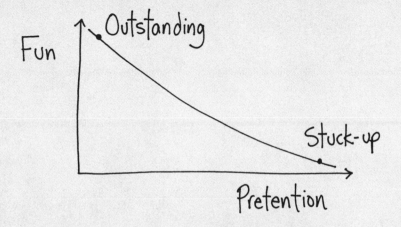

Irony gets in the way of experience. Drop the
pretense, and you'll have room to carry the day.

Sing along to cheesy pop music.
Enjoy things that are out of style.
Make silly faces. Stop stifling your giggles.

Give yourself permission to enjoy yourself.

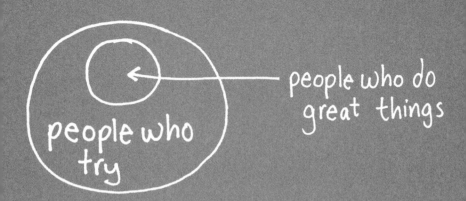

people who do
great things

people who
try

Give yourself

people who are never
invited to parties

some credit.

You deserve a chance.
You deserve to have fun.
You deserve to be happy.
You've got abilities &
curiosities & things to offer.
So go on, jump in there.

Not only is there room for you,
there's a need for you.
Really.

Ditch the JUNK.

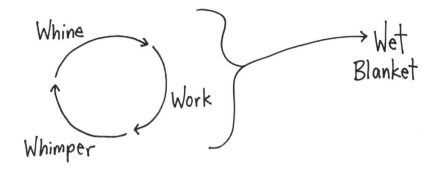

Not every activity is worthwhile.

Not every dreadful task is mandatory.

Avoid the things that drag you down and make you weary. And if you must do them (laundry, taxes), then do them with gusto and put them out of your mind. You'll have more room for what matters. More room for what's interesting.

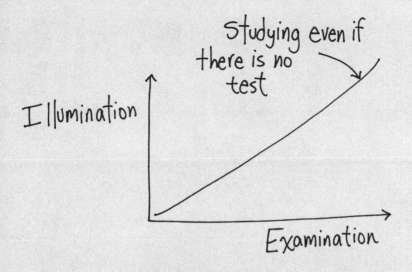

Start with a wonder. How does this work?

What makes that happen? Then poke.

Take things apart and put them back together.

Push buttons. Change settings.

See how the pieces fit. See what powers

the engine. See how interesting it all is.

Find yourself

Noble

Powerful

Lonely

↑

Batman
—or—
The lady at the
DMV

Seek someone who makes you smile.
Someone who lives the way you want to.
Someone you admire. Someone real and
imperfect.

a hero.

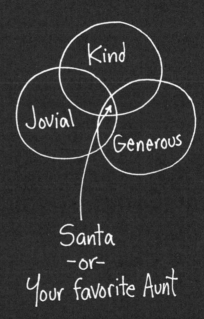

Kind

Jovial

Generous

Santa
—or—
Your favorite Aunt

Learn from them two things:

1. What they do well

2. What they do not do so well

Defend what you Love.

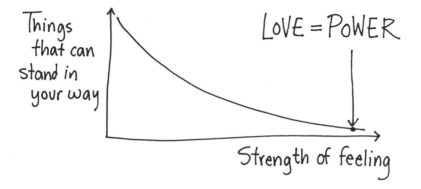

You have treasured people, places, and things.

They are precious and powerful. Fight for them.

Don't just let them lounge in the back of your mind.

A love ignored will wither and die.

Own your territory.

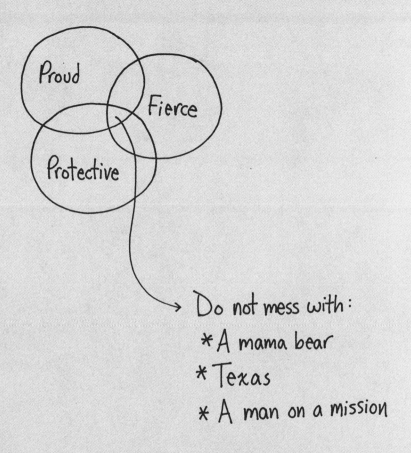

Proud

Fierce

Protective

Do not mess with:
* A mama bear
* Texas
* A man on a mission

Whatever you're doing, enjoy it. Embrace it.
Master it as well as you can. Own it.
This is how to combine a sense of freedom
with a feeling of safety.

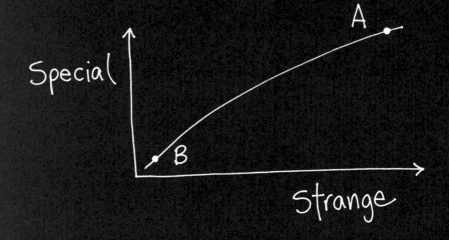

Special

A

B

Strange

A = Well-known
B = Well-behaved

Step 4

Embrace your weirdness.

No one is normal.
Everyone has quirks and
insights unique to themselves.
Don't hide these things—
they are what make you
interesting.

ALTER the uniform.

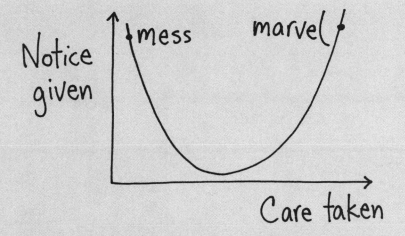

Dress up. Dress down. Grab a pail for the seashore.
Put on a hat only you like. Put on what makes
you feel like yourself.

Sometimes the right pair of shoes can make you feel
better in your own skin.

conformity

invisibility

monotony

Be yourself
in PUBLIC.

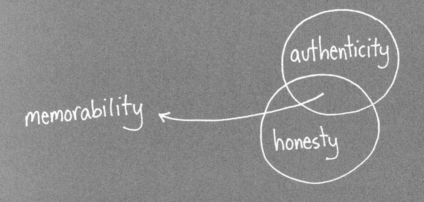

authenticity

memorability

honesty

Leave the house as yourself.
Be yourself at work.
Wear your personality
PROUDLY.

Don't censor your skills
or hide your unique features.
To have a difference is
to have an identity.
To make it public is
to be truly yourself.

DO NOT

Difficulty
breathing ↑ •Asthma

•Feeling free

Costumes. Poses. False smiles and
forced conformity. It all gets in the way
of what's truly interesting.

FAKE IT.

- Feeling trapped

- Hazmat

→

Weight of mask

You are innately unique: There's no
need to hide behind an ill-fitting mask.

wrong

weird

No more apologizing.

Hiding
what's special

You are not wrong to be unique.
You not incorrect because you are
different. You should not be sorry for
being interesting.

Smile
at
Sneers.

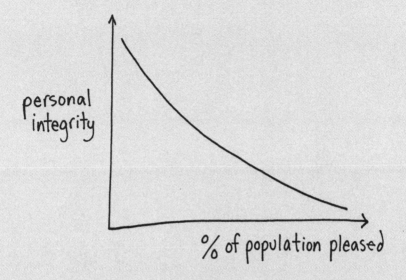

personal
integrity

% of population pleased

Not everyone will understand you.

Not everyone will appreciate you.

Not everyone will embrace you.

Do not change for them. Just smile at them,
and move along.

Stand PROUD

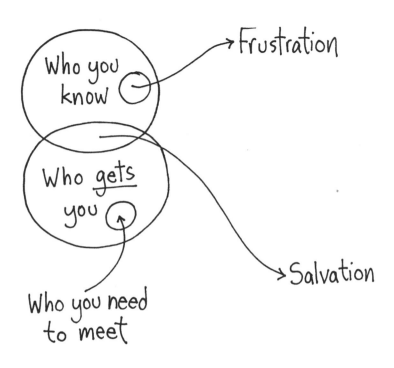

Your weirdness is a valuable thing.

A badge of honor. A point of pride.

It sets you apart and helps you find other people

who will revel in your presence—and you in theirs.

Question Your MOTIVES.

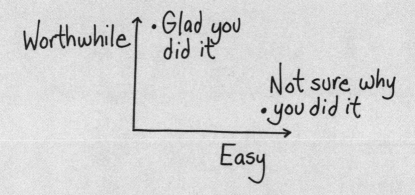

Interesting people are motivated by things bigger than the status quo. Are you doing what someone else expects you to, or what you feel, deep down, that you must do?

The only way to exceed expectations is to ignore them—and do what needs doing instead.

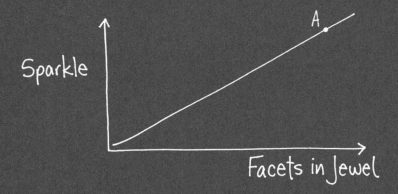

Sparkle

Facets in Jewel

A

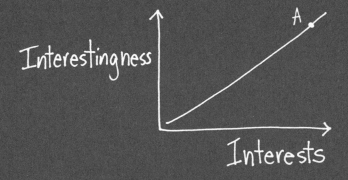

Interestingness

Interests

A

A = Brilliant

get SIDETRACKED.

Who's more interesting: A famous scientist, or the famous scientist who plays the cello and whittles marionettes in a lighthouse at the edge of the world where he sometimes writes poetry by the light of passing ships?

Exactly. Follow your weird impulses and do all sorts of things. Getting sidetracked can lead you to exactly where you belong.

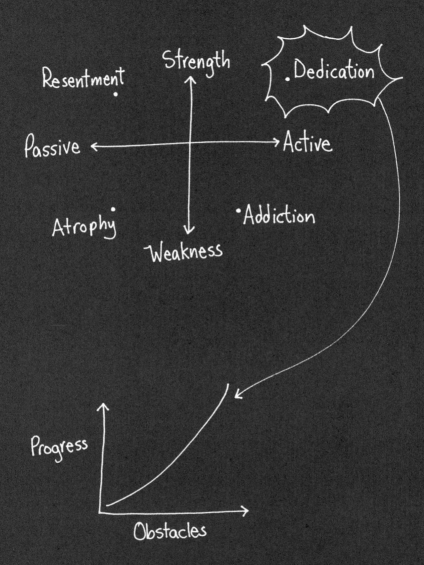

Keep moving.

Every day, make another move toward what makes you happy. Take another step toward adventure. Let another piece of your special sort of weirdness out.

Before you know it, you'll be in a very different place—a far more interesting place.

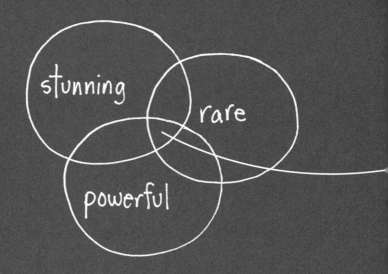

stunning

rare

powerful

FOSTER the

Encourage the uniqueness of others.
Support what's odd. Put your money
where the weird is. Spend time
doing what's different, strange, or
amazingly odd.

Obvious
talent
-or-
being struck
by lightning

DIFFERENCES.

The world expects compliance, and
wonderful weirdos need all the help
they can get.

CAPITALIZE on your QUIRKS.

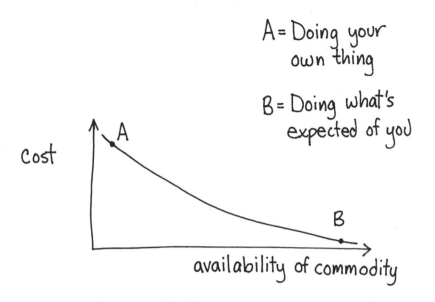

A = Doing your own thing

B = Doing what's expected of you

Cost (y-axis)

availability of commodity (x-axis)

What makes you interesting makes you valuable:
Only you can express what you know,
do what you do, and know what you know.
You don't need a giant niche, just one big enough
to plant a flag in.

Find your

Things
to run
from

•Fear

Don't run away and join the rat race.
Run away and join a circus full of people
who are living their dreams.

CIRCUS.

.Reality

.Hope

→

Things to run toward

If you seek a circus, you'll be running toward something enjoyable, instead of merely exhausting yourself.

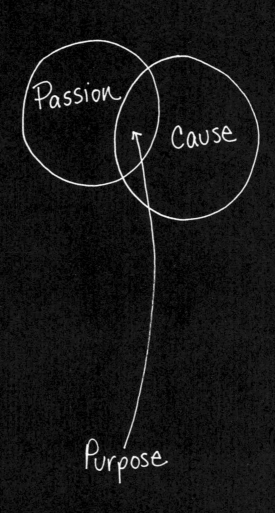

Step 5

Have a CAUSE.

If you don't give a
damn about anything,
no one will give a damn
about you.

Recall what makes you CRY.

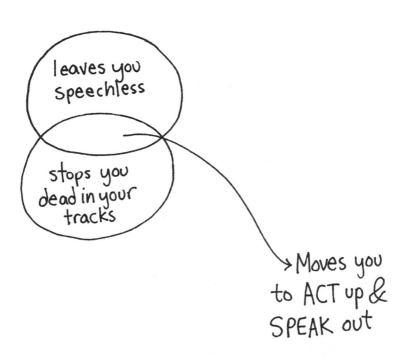

leaves you speechless

stops you dead in your tracks

→ Moves you to ACT up & SPEAK out

A place. A person.
A creature. A song.
Now devote a little more of yourself
to that memory.

Give

Receive

Give

→ Tax breaks for charitable donations & Functional Relationships

Selfishly.

It feels good to be kissed back.
It feels great to give gifts. It feels
spectacular to be a catalyst to the
happiness of someone else. Being
generous is disgustingly satisfying.

Spend
money
like it's worth
Something.

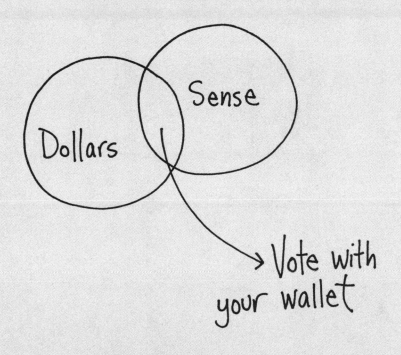

Dollars

Sense

Vote with your wallet

Who gets your cash? Where do you get it?
What people and companies are involved?
Do you agree with their politics, practices, and
behaviors? And is that all okay with you?
If not, know you can always make change
with your money.

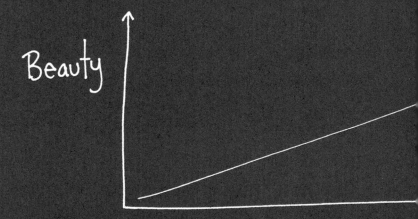

Beauty

Spectators do not make news.

Observers do not steer history. Be vulnerable.

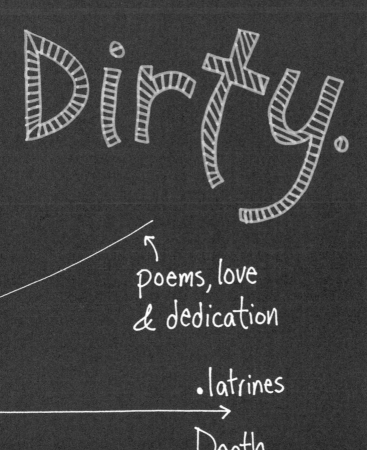

Dirty.

poems, love
& dedication

• latrines

Depth

Be serious. Be immersed.
If you want to matter, you have to climb all the
way into the mess that is before you.

SpeAk UP.

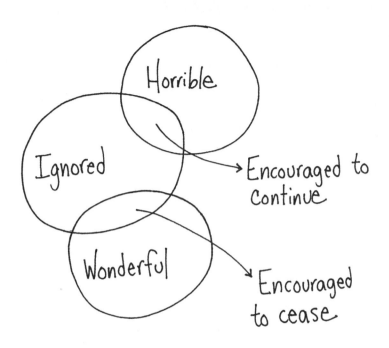

Praise the marvelous. Shut down the nasty.

Articulate what others are afraid to say out loud.

Further the discourse.

decent

passable

typical

Do the

> No one writes
songs about this.

best good.

Ask yourself: Is this the best that's possible? Then ask: Well, what is?

And spend your time working on that.

Risk ORDINARY for GREAT.

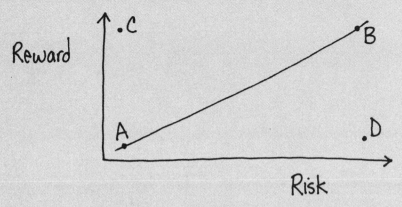

A = Boredom
B = A biography worth reading
C = Ponzi scheme sales pitch
D = Danger

Feel greater than fine. Do better than just okay.
Amazing is rare, if only because so few people reach
for it. Risking the ordinary is the only way to get
something extraordinary.

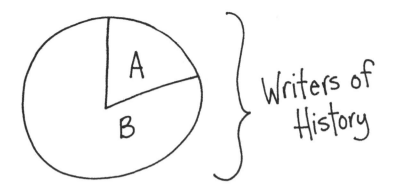

A = The self-appointed winners
B = Ghostwriters hired by A

You are the protagonist and author of your
life's story. Perfect? No one is. Compelling?
We all can be, if our hearts drive the plot.
Be a character worthy of the ages.

ANYTHING is better THAN NOTHING.

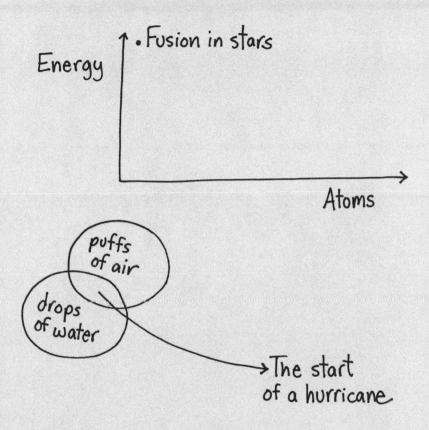

Actions matter. Even small ones.

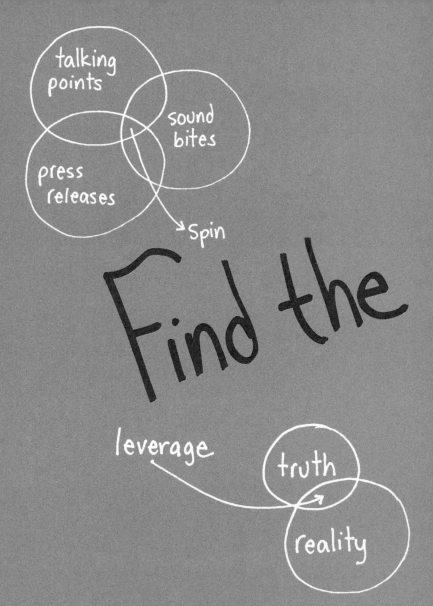

talking points

sound bites

press releases

Spin

Find the

leverage

truth

reality

fulcrum.

Below the obvious, behind the superficial, under the excuses & facades, you will find the crux of the matter.

Work from that point.

Proper leverage gets a hell of a lot of work done.

PUT IT ALL

A = Everything makes sense
B = Everything stresses you out

IN ORDER.

B

Priorities

Give what is important precedence.
Everything else will arrange itself.

Set tables & Examples.

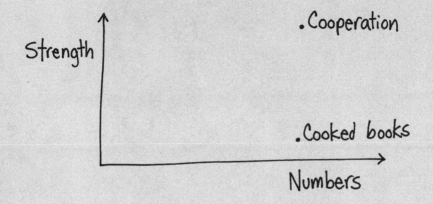

Bring together as many people as you can
to help you. Share your energy.
Share your ideas. Share your cause.

And make sure you have plenty of cake.
Everyone loves cake.

Minimize the Swagger.

Egos get in the way of ideas.
If your arrogance is more
obvious than your expertise,
you are someone other
people avoid.

The
Universe

*

.

Imagine
Everything

Everything you'll ever know is only a fraction
of a microscopic dribble in the great, churning
universe of information.

All human
knowledge

*Not to scale—I'd need a circle the
size of the solar system to be even
close to accurate.

You do NOT
Know.

Let this humbling fact be comforting in
its enormity.

Just

. Speaking

Noise

To what is said and what is left out.

To the messages between the words.

To the tone of voice.

To the sarcasm and to the reverence.

Listen.

.Listening

→

Understanding

Communication is far more
than just words.

Drop the Titles

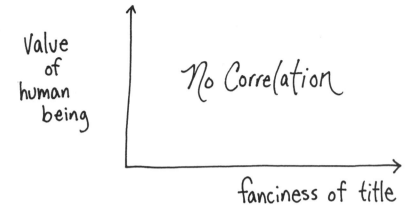

Kings and Queens.

Doctors and Lawyers.

Popes and Mayors and Fishmongers.

Prostitutes and Librarians.

It's not the title that matters;

it's the person behind it.

Not everyone
WANTS
what you
HAVE.

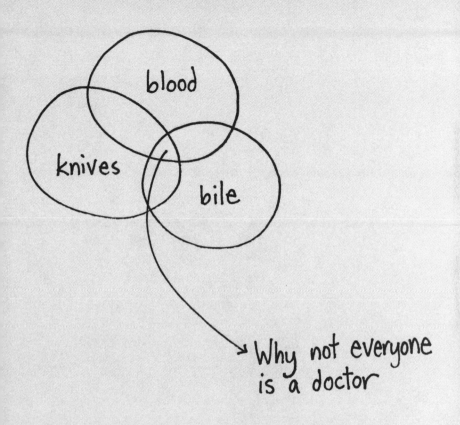

Why not everyone is a doctor

Your greatest accomplishments, no matter how impressive you think them to be, are someone else's worst nightmare. Your most prized possession is another man's disgusting chunk of trash. Be careful what you brag about.

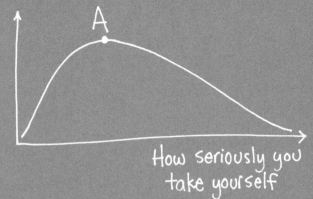

How much others enjoy your presence

A

How seriously you take yourself

Imagine your

A = Not a clown & not a snot

own caricature.

Your nose. Your walk.
Your hair. Your teeth.
Your house. Your school.
Your middle name.
They're actually pretty funny,
if you think about them.
Don't take yourself
too seriously.

Ask more

Ponder

Question

Change
your mind

Questions.

How to get:
A = Smarter
B = Kicked out of the cult

Interesting people are interested in things other than themselves. They're educationally omnivorous. And so they end a lot of sentences with honest question marks.

Strength

RemAin A

Hearts & Brains

Exercise

Student.

Sign up to learn things. Philosophy,
archery, accounting, painting, diving,
fire eating—anything you can admit
you do not understand. You never know
when you'll need a random skill.

Practice VICARIOUS Pride.

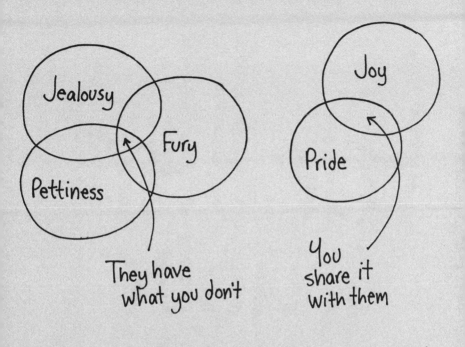

Jealousy

Fury

Pettiness

They have
what you don't

Joy

Pride

You
share it
with them

Have you ever been overwhelmingly proud of
someone other than yourself? If you have,
you know how buoyant and uplifting it feels.

If you haven't, you need to get close enough
to someone to try.

Ponder your Luck.

Situations beyond your control

actions you took

How we all got to THIS exact moment

Do you deserve what you have? Maybe a little.
What you don't have? Probably not.

Acknowledge the roles coincidence, chance,
systemic processes (and yes, maybe even luck)
play in our world.

Admit  GOOFS

Mistakes happen. Often.
Sometimes they're your fault and
sometimes they're your misfortune.

Freely admit to both kinds.

BE A

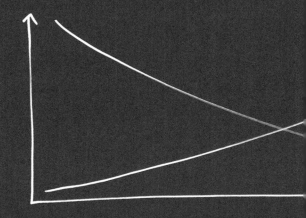

New
Heights
Reached

To everyone you meet. Be the helper,
the adviser, the assistant the hero cannot
do without.

SIDEKICK.

Brings out the best

Fosters the worst

Enablers

Fame and value aren't as closely related as you think.

Be impressed
before you
try to be
IMPRESSIVE.

Majesty. Glory. Beauty.

Balance. Wisdom.

The more often you are amazed, the better your odds of being amazing. Really: How will you know how high to aim if you've never looked up?

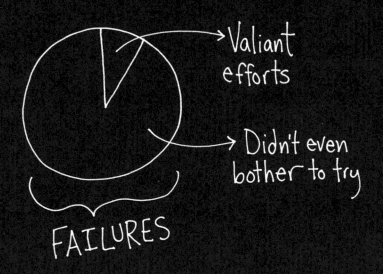

Valiant efforts

Didn't even bother to try

FAILURES

Give it a Shot.

Try it out. Play around with a new idea. Do something strange. If you never leave your comfort zone, you won't grow.

Think abundance

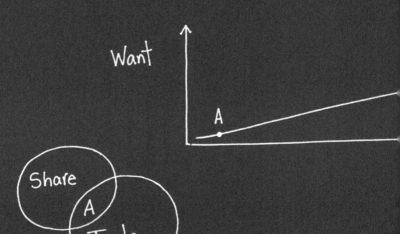

Not Scarcity.

Hoard

B

Consume

B

Greed

If you decide that there is more than
enough to go around, you'll find that
you're correct. The inverse is also true.

worst-
case
scenario

best-
laid
plans

WHY

Don't let this
worry stop you

NOT?

Afraid to fail?

Afraid to fail and that other people might find

out about it? So what if you fail?

Really: So what if you fail?

Would that really be so bad?

ADMIT YOU WANT TO.

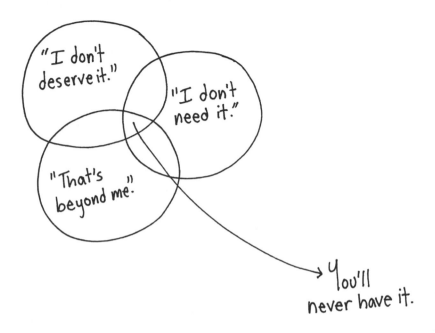

To deny a dream is to kill it in its infancy.

Don't feel guilty for taking a shot at something.
Don't feel terrible for wanting something.

Save the guilt for never giving yourself
the chance to try.

SURPRISE YOURSELF.

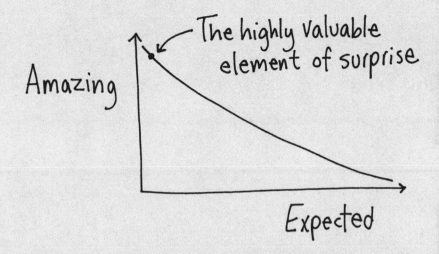

Amazing

The highly valuable element of surprise

Expected

What's expected of you?

Try something else. What's the next step?

Take a different one.

Typical isn't mandatory, after all.

Stockpile

What you talk about

↑ • Boorish

• Unfortunate

Read randomly. Overhear on purpose.
Watch movies and clouds and people.

anecdotes.

·Interesting

·Shy

⟶

What you know about

The more you absorb, the more you
can exude.

Overstep your BOUNDS.

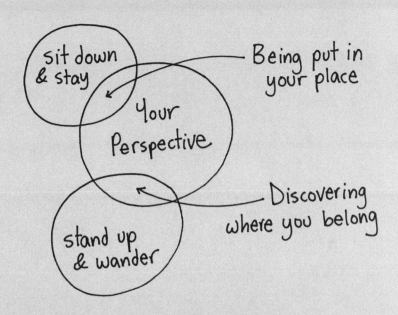

Just because you've never been somewhere
doesn't mean you don't belong.
Just because it's not in your job description
doesn't mean you can't do it. Only you can really
decide what league you really belong in.

GIVE YOURSELF PERMISSION.

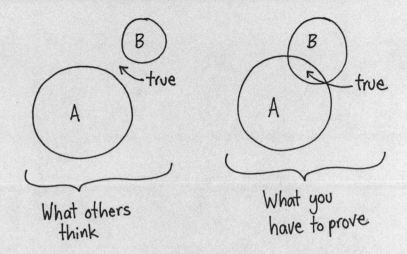

A = What's Possible
B = Your WILD Dream

Need permission?

Give it to yourself, because most of the time,

nobody else will.

Joy $\left\{ \vphantom{\begin{matrix}A\\B\end{matrix}} \right.$

A = The task at hand
B = Your heart

Volunteer

for the job.

Say, "Yes, I will be there for you."

Show up, ready for anything.

Put your heart into it.

This is how people begin to fall in love

with you, and you with your work.

Make REAL

Actions ↑ •Impulsive

Maybe tomorrow?

I guess I'll start later?

No, make your plans kinetic, not potential.

PLANS.

.Strategic

.Hesitant

→

Plans

Procrastination leads to regret.

Declare Your Affecti♡ns

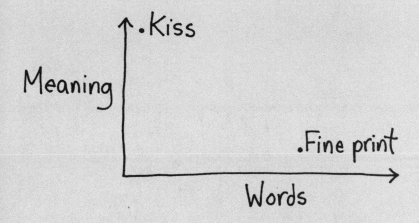

It takes a very brave person to be emotionally vulnerable. It takes a strong spirit to go weak in the knees.

Interesting people are characters in interesting love stories.

TACKLE the HARD STUFF.

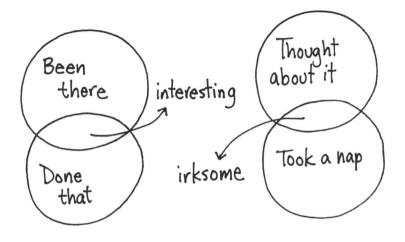

Know that obstacles scare away most of the competition. And that the hardest things are the things that are the most satisfying to be done with.

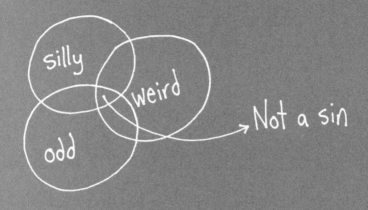

Silly

weird

odd

→ Not a sin

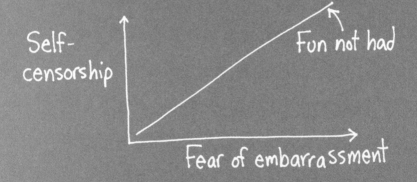

Self-censorship

Fun not had

Fear of embarrassment

Have no Shame.

Sing badly and loudly.
Skip down the street.
Go to that open mic night.
Uncensor your personality.
More people will smile
than laugh,
and if they laugh,
that's their sad problem.

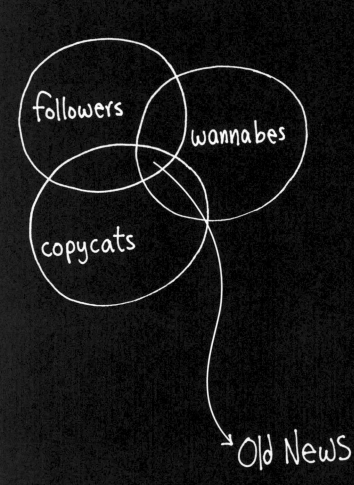

Hop off the bandwagon.

If everyone else is doing it, you're already late to the party. Do your own thing, and others will hop onto the spiffy wagon you built yourself.

Don't confuse
a tradition
with a mandate.

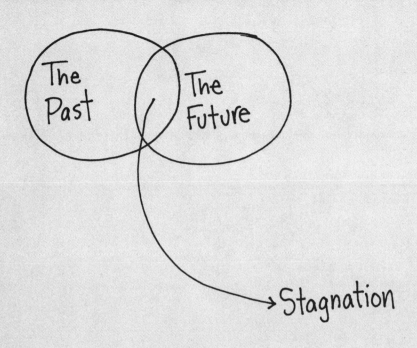

So that's how it's always been done?

That's "just the way it is"?

We just have to deal with it?

No, not anymore.

Do a VERY

People
who do it
for a
living

so many things

Ever sit in traffic and wonder what everyone else sitting in traffic does for a living?
For a hobby? For fun?

ODD JOB.

How often you hear about it

There are as many answers as there are people. They're all possibilities.

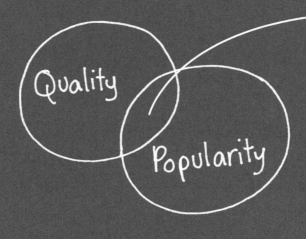

Question

→Not
NECESSARILY

Ubiquity.

Just because it's everywhere
doesn't mean it's good or
worth participating in.

FOLLOW *your* CURIOSITY.

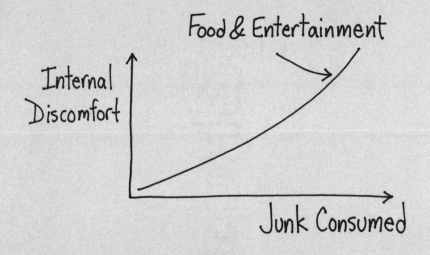

If you find yourself drowning in the vat
of popular but boring sludge, your curiosity
will be your lifeline.

Crawl into

NICHES

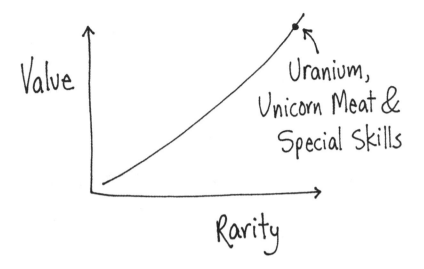

The smaller the niche, the less room there is for copycats.

If you want to be interesting, work with specifics, not generics.

Be the next
whatever-sized
thing.

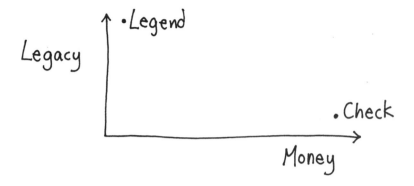

You don't have to be world famous or
filthy rich to be successful.

You simply have to do what you do best.

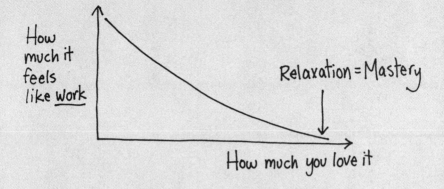

Unlink stress and success.

Find the work that satisfies you, and

you might just avoid a heart attack or three.

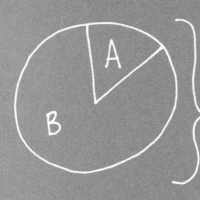

Runners in rat race

CHANGE

A = Slightly ahead
B = Far behind
C = Winners

MEASUREMENTs.

Square footage? Horsepower?
Millions in the bank?
People in your fan club?
Days you wake up happy?
Look at what you're
measuring and consider
alternative units.

Start your

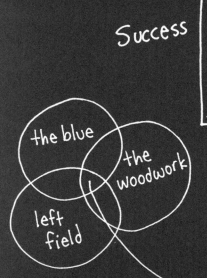

Success

the blue

the woodwork

left field

Where ideas
come from
(when your mind is
ready for them)

own craze.

it doesn't matter where you begin

How far you go

Every cultural phenomenon starts as
an idea. When you have one, do what you
can to take it from the corner of your
mind to the public. The whole world just
might embrace it.

Leave the Safety of Home.

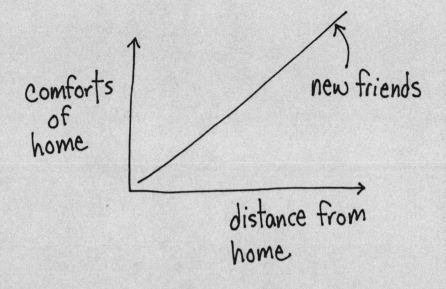

You grew up with certain people who did
certain things in certain places.
Leave home to see how unique *and*
universal your childhood was.

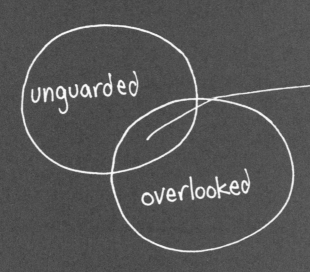

Take over

→ Undervalued
people,
places
& things

unclaimed
Spaces.

When the powers that be overlook
something, you can take that something
over and become a power that is.

INVESTIGATE
the
OBSCURE.

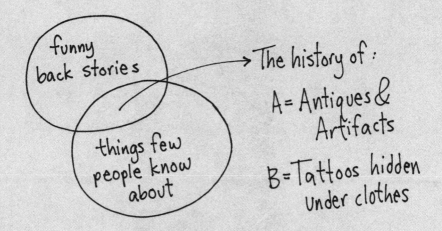

The history of :

A = Antiques & Artifacts

B = Tattoos hidden under clothes

Revive forgotten stories.

Read old books. Dust off forgotten trends.

Listen to rare music.

You might find your favorite thing

hiding in the woodwork.

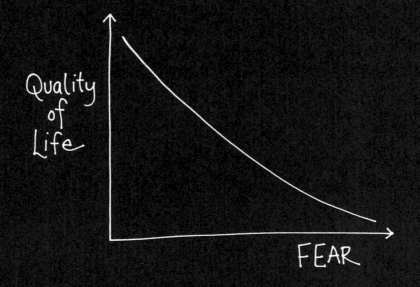

Step 9

Grow a pair.

Bravery is needed to have
contrary opinions and to take
unexpected paths. If you're not
courageous, you're going to
be hanging around the water-
cooler, talking about the guy
who actually is.

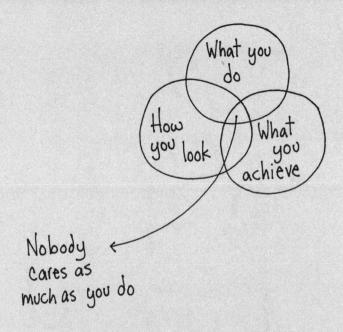

If you have a personal dream or a wish
or a desire, know that you're the only one
who gives enough damns to see it realized.

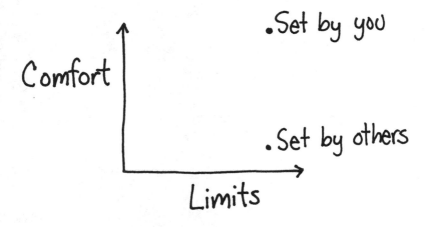

If you find yourself working for something
that feels pointless or fruitless, stop.
Don't fight for anything you don't see value in.
You'll be surprised how many others join you
in the protest.

Avoid

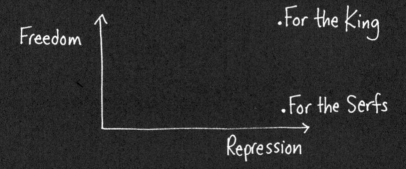

In order to do interesting things, you need
to have the freedom to explore, experiment,
and innovate.

AUTHORITY.

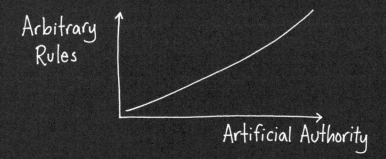

Arbitrary Rules

Artificial Authority

Authorities mainly work to confine, contain, and limit such behavior.

Work around that as much as possible.

ACCEPT
Friction

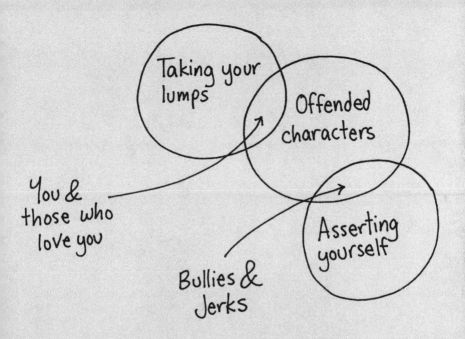

You don't want to impose.

You may shy away from making waves.

You may feel like you couldn't dare to ask

for what you need. You need to get

over that.

Stress

Not so easy
after all

Safe
is often

Challenges

DANGEROUS.

An easy life is like quicksand:
Before you know it, you're trapped
and can't move, can't breathe, can't
get to where you really wanted to go.
Don't coast unless you're rolling
downhill on a bicycle.

GET

unstoppable
force

immovable
object

STUBBORN.

Somebody who gets things done

Giving up is boring. Getting frustrated and plowing ahead despite it all requires the power that only a truly interesting person possesses.

Lobotomize culturally INSANE practices.

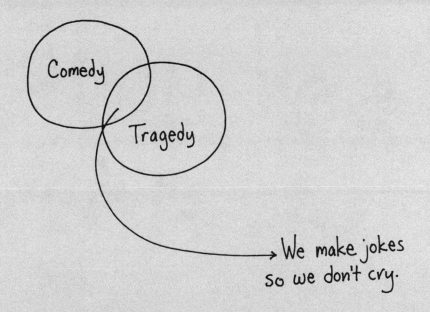

Society has been known to burn witches.

Slavery was legal once, too.

What else is going on that needs to be put right?

And what are you going to do about it?

SET YOUR OWN

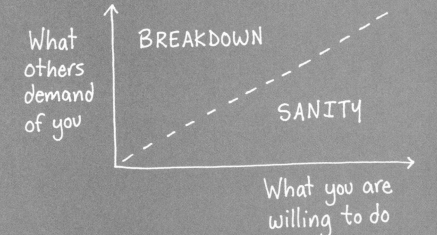

What others demand of you

What you are willing to do

BREAKDOWN

SANITY

BOUNDARIES.

On time. On attention.
On money. On love.
And defend your territory
from those who want to
knock down the walls
that keep you sane.

Get ~~REJECTED~~ A LOT

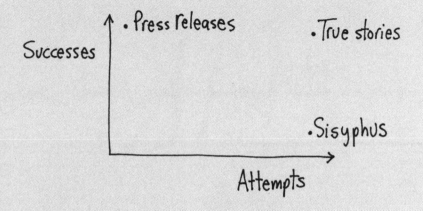

When you put yourself out there, a lot of people will reject, dismiss, or ignore you. But a few will embrace and champion you. While the nos may sting, only the yeses matter.

MAKe A Mess.

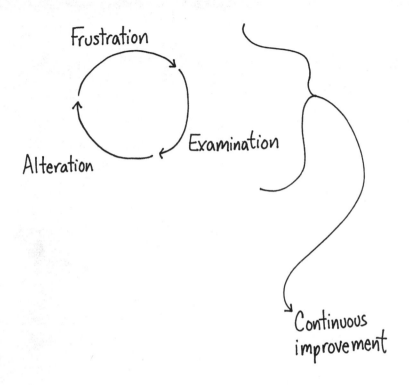

Frustration

Examination

Alteration

Continuous
improvement

Rearrange furniture, elements, ideas, and
opportunities. Then put the pieces back into
a different and better order. It's time to put
the creativity back into creative destruction.

Whine

Problem
Resolution

If things are unsatisfactory:
1) Document them.
2) Change them.

Few people ever bother with that
second bit.

Productively.

•A

•B

→

Inarticulate Wailing

A = Babies   B = Adults

WIELD SHARP WORDS.

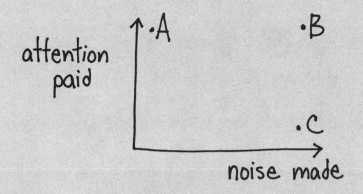

A = Compelling argument
B = Sirens & Bombs
C = Ranting

"Your tongue is a weapon kept sharp with use."
—An anonymous smart person

Choose your words wisely.

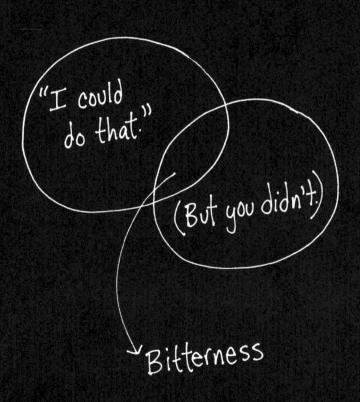

Ignore the Scolds.

Boring is safe, and you will be told to behave yourself. The scolds could have, would have, should have. But they didn't. And they resent you for your adventures.

JETTISON **Toxic** CARGO

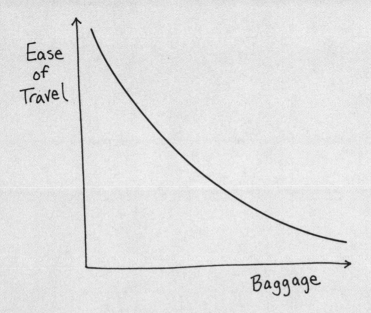

If you've got bad memories attached to places, things, and even people: Let them go. You will feel lighter almost immediately.

Avoid people
who make
you feel
CRAPPY.

Small

icky

annoying

→ Household
pests
&
the people they
remind you of

Don't return their calls or take their antagonistic bait.
The only way to win their game is to quit
playing along. Besides, no one is fascinated by
your constant irritation.

Don't be
MEAN
to yourself.

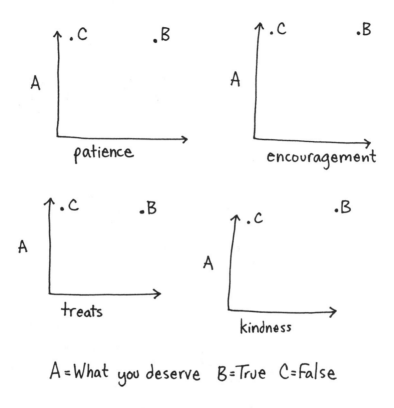

A = What you deserve B = True C = False

The heinous little voice inside your head that puts you down and wears you out? Shut it up with actions that prove it wrong. Caution: This may take years.

Don't TAKE
ADVICE
from people you
Don't RESPECT.

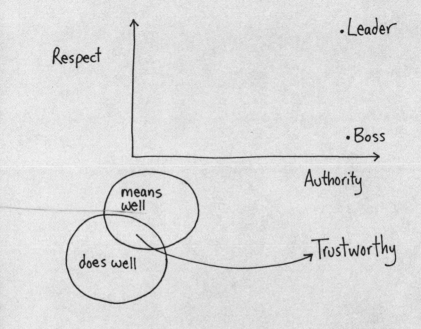

Unless you want to turn out like them. Which you
obviously don't.

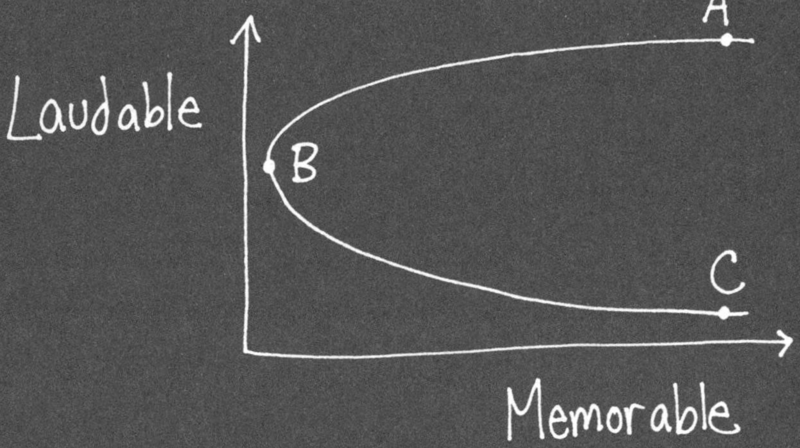

Learn from

A = Genius
B = Perfect attendance
C = Criminal

ALL examples.

You can learn how not to live by
occasionally interacting with jerks.
You can learn how to live from paying
attention to people you admire.

Think of it as behavioral research.

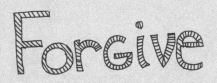

Forgive

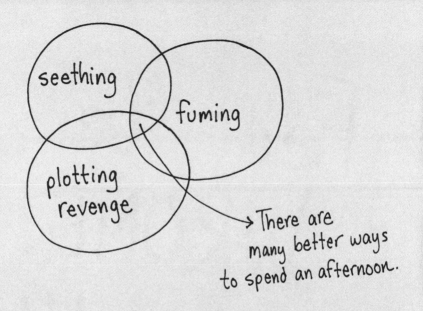

seething

fuming

plotting
revenge

→ There are
many better ways
to spend an afternoon.

Most people, even the nasty ones, are doing
the best they can. They may not deserve your love
and admiration, but your scorn burns the both
of you.

Fear the WRONG DESTINY.

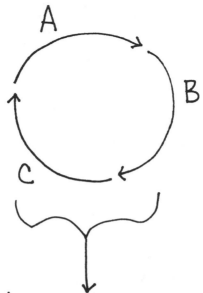

How to ensure you
do not accomplish anything

A = Wish for something to happen
B = Wait for someone else to bring it to you
C = Curse the darkness

Waiting around for a sign?
Sorry, you have to paint your own.

Don't confuse taunts with critiques.

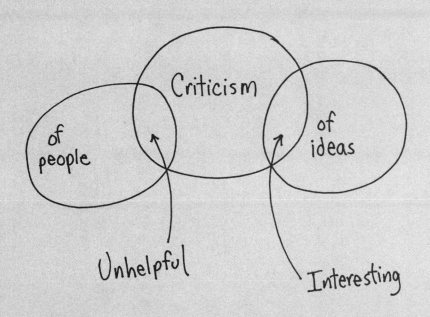

It's only constructive if you can use it
to get better.

TRUST YOUR

Application

FOSTERED

TALENTS.

WASTED

Talent →

Whoever said you just weren't
(_____) *enough* was an ass.
And they were wrong.

Belligerently
ADVANCE.

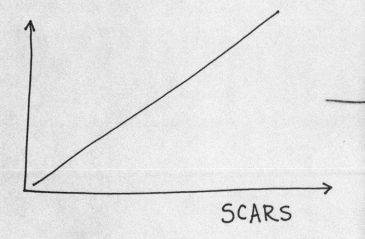

Proof you've been alive

SCARS

Maybe your past isn't perfect. Maybe it was brutal.

Maybe you were brutal. Maybe you've got

more scars than you thought one skin could hold.

You can't linger on those thoughts.

You will drown in them.

After all, it's only an interesting backstory if you

can get past it.

Ponder the

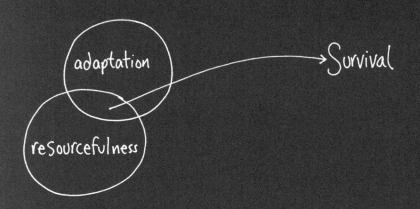

adaptation → Survival

resourcefulness

The platypus is a beast cobbled from
seemingly leftover parts. Yet it thrives and
it's amazingly unique. Don't be afraid to
cobble together your own functional set of
interesting assets.

Platypus.

Pretty

·A   ·B

·C

Smart

A = Eaten by predators
B = More girls than you think
C = Heimlich Maneuver

Give Extra Chances—
ESPECIALLY
to yourself

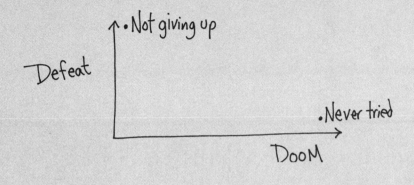

If you're not dead, you can still change things.

In Summary:

Adventurous
Generous
Active
Strange
Caring
Humble
Daring
Original
Brave
+ Self-Assured
_____

Interesting

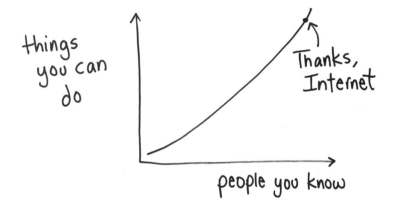

things
you can
do

Thanks,
Internet

people you know

Acknowledgments

Thanks, admiration, and industrial-sized vats of
goodness go out to Ted Weinstein, my uber-agent
who offered to help me before I even knew I needed
him; to Noah Iliinsky, who champions my work like
it's something I pay him to do; to Sunni Brown, my
fellow doodle bug and voice of bravery; to Bruce
Tracy, my wise and gentle editor who works with so
much heart; and to the entire staff at *Forbes*, for the
chance to share my work on such a broad platform.
I am disgustingly fortunate to be able to work with
all of you.

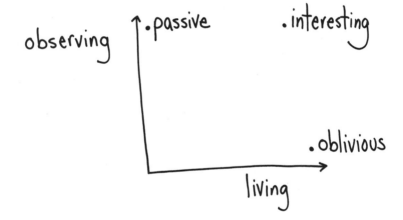